Poetry's Poesy Vol.1 Scattered Thoughts

Brooks Crittenton

ROYAL MEDIA
AND PUBLISHING LLC

BLESSINGS
2
THE MOST HIGH!

Royal Media and Publishing
P. O. Box 4321
Jeffersonville, IN 47131
502-802-5385
http://royamediaandpublishing.com
royalmediapublishing@gmail.com

Cover Design: Gad Elite Book Covers

ISBN-13: 978-0-9987154-7-6

Printed in the United States of America

Dedication

I give thanks to the Most High for giving me this talent & the words to say.

My mother Dawn Graham for being that backbone for me and mental support. I appreciate you.

This book goes to those who stayed by my side. My wife, my daughter & my kinfolk for being true regardless of how things got.

My brothers & sisters for being that everyday balance I need in my life.

To all those who've had an impact in my life guiding me to success.

I want to dedicate this to all of the love ones who are no longer here, I love y'all.

Table of Contents

Introduction

Poetry's Poesy Vol.1 "<u>Scattered Thoughts</u>" is a collection of poems for spiritual healing. Brooks "Poetry" Crittenton has been writing poems since his 2005 freshman year in high school. High Tech High Media Arts which was funded by Oprah Winfrey & Bill Gates is located in San Diego. This high school provided this young poet an inspirational teacher named Diana Sanchez to introduce him to poetry.

As a teacher, she gave Brooks three spoken word mentors Rudy Francisco, Ant Black & Kendrick Dial all who inspired him in different ways. These poets collectively are called Collective Purpose. Collective Purpose & Diana gave Brooks his first opportunity performing at their open mic venue named Elevated. In 2009, Brooks had an opportunity to teach a young poet Milan Finnie the art of poetry his senior year.

As the teaching went on & their relationship grew, this student blessed him with the name Poetry and he never looked back. In 2010, Brooks joined the United States Marines. As he served the military &

law enforcement he continued to write poems and express himself artistically. In 2015, he took that year to start his spiritual rebirth and understand himself and his writings as well as why he was chosen to be called poetry. In 2017, it was the peak of his spiritual journey he refers to having a connection with the Most High. After preparation he is now ready to share his poetic views with others.

Poesy

I've grown in your artform
I have given you my heart,
so, my old self will be reborn
The start was rocky,
mentors taught me
I've stumbled in this journey
I'm not perfect,
you instilled patience
I need it urgent,
tired of looking in eyes who's waiting
this platform, gave dream chasing
back breaking, mind shaking
You gave love when needed
You held my secrets
Offered tools to fight my demons
Poesy
I've grown in your artform
I have given you my heart,
so, my old self will be reborn

1.*Thoughts*

I have stuff on my mind
The stuff that is on my mind is not kind
Let me rewind
Back to the beginning of my thoughts
I better say what I got to say
Because I may not be here another day
I feel like I'm in a boxing match with my thoughts
They're swinging blows to my chest with no rest
People think I'm lethal,
Even when I walk in these streets with my du-rag &
I sag
People try to judge me
but how the hell can you judge me
I keep thinking why do I have to act
Like this or that, so I can be called black
That shit is wack
I refuse to fit into the stereotype
Sometimes my thoughts sink like the titanic & I
panic
Because I got a taste of what the
United Negro College Foundation said,
"That the mind is a terrible thing to waste."
So, I keep thinking I should be a young black boy,
getting an education
So, when I grow up I'll be grown black man
Getting a promotion
& after all this my mind will be at peace.

2. ***Effects of Love***

Look, she has come by once in my lifetime
Showing me things & blowing my mind
Imposters try to be you
But can't do the things you do
Things she says is true, this girl will never lie to you
This girl will wrap you in her arms but
Never bring you harm
For her she will mention
that she's here for good intentions
This feeling this girl got,
got to be an alien
Because it's out of this world
Now she's willing to do anything for this dude
But took me by surprise, had me a little confused
This thing this girl is doing i need to know if it's a
game
Because she's giving me the world
& I don't even know her name
It's weird kuz when she gone, I can feel the pain
& now can understand songs like
Can you stand the rain
Now she got my heart leaping, me feining
Being in a white box room SCREAMING
At the top of lungs
Doctors walk past, look and laugh
Saying I'm still too young
Me not seeing her is driving my weak
But it's only been a couple of weeks

Now they released me back into these streets
Not seeing her, I cannot speak
Wait this girl transformed herself into a needle
So, I can inject herself into me
Felt so good, like life should
But I guess that was the peak or the point
Like smoking your last joint, it goes downhill
Emotions all over the place like my body had a spill
That night her, she oh I wanted to kill
Before I could do it I choked.
Woke up with a note saying
You cannot get rid of me that easily I will be back
for you trust me
Signed L.O.V.E

3. _What Do You Call It?_

I am arm, leg, leg, arm & head
God's sitting at the same table breaking bread
Since birth we've been told our worth
Falling in love with Earth
Earth, the black queen, the first provider of life
Sitting next to me, sipping on wine
She, listening to knowledge
I'm listening to wisdom
As we are connecting, we are overstanding
I am arm, leg, leg, arm & head
No longer will I accept the bullshit you have fed
I cannot ignore all these tears that have been shed
Transforming mentalities about my community,
that we come from monkeys
Scared to share the truth, that we come from
royalty, hiding our history
Will not dare speak on Black Wall St
36 blocks bombed on American soil
military airborne, black families torn
How many more Mothers do we have to see mourn
I am arm, leg, leg, arm & head
Mother Earth in my ear saying,
"Love is what I need to spread
 hate is keeping my brothers & sistas dead "
Blinded, everyday I'm reminded, it's clear
Our screams don't reach the Government's ear
They have our future leaders, living in fear
"YOU ARE ABLE TO DO ANYTHING."

Is the only thing I want my kids to hear
I am Arm, Leg, Leg, Arm & Head

4. _Cain_

Am I my brother's keeper?
Why are you asking
I'm attending to my soil, trying to plant my seeds
How can you ask me of another man,
that's not next to me
Even though same blood pump through veins
Our relationship is strange
How can my little brother be glorified,
you would be mortified
If you knew the thoughts I have "I'm Serious"
Where is my brother? It's a secret
No contact for obvious reasons,
been plenty of seasons
Since we sat at the same table eating
Parents teaching, God's reason, believe me
Every Wednesday, every Friday, every Sunday
We in church, learning his words
He's doing everything right, it's getting on my
nerves
I've heard you not supposed to have
jealousy, envy
Everything my birthright deserves
He's getting, he's receiving
Something in the back of my head
Saying "Stay away from these demons"
The more I think about this, I ball my fist
Tell my brother, I'm going to teach you defense
While I swing these hits

He screams "Please bruh quit"
That look on his face
Would be something I could never forget
My anger comes from,
your perfect gifts, the sacrifices you give,
Time you invested
These moments I relive, I can't forgive
Because my offering was never accepted
I HATE YOU!!!! For taking my blessing
"Where is your brother?"
Don't you hear me confessing, my profession
"WHERE IS YOUR BROTHER?"
Okay I'll answer your question
Last time I remember we were jesting
Wrong words were exchanged, I started stressing
He tried to walk away, then we started wrestling
"WHAT have you done?"
I couldn't tell my parents
Had to pack my bags & start stepping
With every stride I started reflecting
With every breath I started regretting, kuz
"Where is your brother?"
Was God's only question

5. _Felicia_

I'm going to tell you this story about this young lady
Her whole life to some will feel it's crazy
Some will be outraged trying to fix the problem
because they feel it's not right
Some folk will say shit, that's just our life
Felicia was this young beautiful black girl
Natural hair, couldn't stand to wear a weave
Anything in this world she believed she can be
In the hood, she stayed
had a job that decently paid
& came home with good grades
What else more would her parents want
Acceptance letters from colleges,
first in her family, she was the real deal
BUT....the boyfriend in her life,
gave her dad a bad feel
This is a dude who didn't pay attention in school
Getting in trouble with homies because he decided
to act like a fool
Always in her ear, reciting I'll be here,
with me there should be no fear
They have been dating for about two years
& Still her innocence is as precious as an
Oyster's Pearl
But she knew his birthday was coming up
& What he wanted in the whole wide world
So, she presented him her Oysters Pearl
You know lips to lips, flesh to flesh

When it was all done
She laid there on the mattress
Not knowing how to accept it
After his birthday, He started acting different
No longer will he come over to just listen
All he wanted was flesh to flesh on the mattress
It was a run-on sentence someone forgot to put a period
She crying to God she can't be pregnant
Calling her boyfriend, He acting ignorant
He said "That baby not mine"
She said "How when you was my first time"
He said "Bitch you must've lied, stop calling my phone, leave me alone."
Building enough courage to talk to her parents at home
Telling them "Life isn't fair"
They couldn't afford it,
So, they put they daughter on welfare
The school acted as if they didn't Care about the situation
Teachers didn't Dare pay attention
& The image she once was people started forgetting
Couldn't afford college baby started working
People in her ear,
Why work a 9 to 5 when you can get more twerking
Doing a couple of shows,
Having fun taking off your clothes
It's really nothing to be a shame about
It's not like we never seen what you got
A life decision she had to make on the spot

Kuz money she needed so her son can eat
Felicia threw something nice on,
Went to the saloon and got a weave
Doing an occupation her parents couldn't believe
Doing it for a while she'll tell you the money was aight
All she was doing was
drinking, taking drugs & taking off her clothes all night
Needing more money she started tricking
Reminiscing on the past,
The old self she started missing
Her name went missing when men referred to her as all kind bi***es
I just talked about one girl it's hard to paint a bigger picture
You know I told the story to someone &
They said "I don't believe you"
My reply was "One event can change the path in your life just ask Felicia"

6. _Why_

Why, do you guide my steps
You, watch me rest
When I showed you less
Who am I,
Other than an average being
Walking on thin lines
Drinking away my demons
Trying to clear my mind
I don't know why
You showed me favor
When I was eating at the same ol' table
We were having a conversation & I denied you
We were having a conversation & I didn't want you
We were just having a conversation
Looking around, asking my family where are you?
Sitting on the same damn couch
I'm all by myself
Wait...there's a figure standing in the corner
Swaying back and forth
Looking like he wants to say something
I hear mumbling, mumbling...... blessing
I hear mumbling, mumbling.......blessing
"WHY DO I GUIDE YOUR STEPS
WHEN YOU SHOWED ME LESS
IT'S BECAUSE YOU ARE BLESSED"
I watch you when you rest,
I'm the energy to calm you down,
When you are stressed

I am that new paved path to walk on,
When your life is a mess
"WHY DO I SHOW YOU FAVOR?"
Have you thought,
I might need your vessel for later
To serve my words
To hit a nerve & reach a soul
Whether they're living in their highs or they're lows
You & yours will be protected if you do what you're told
YAH, don't you know, I'm a human of flesh
A man of error
"Yes, I also know your complexed &
Have many layers
I Know Your Heart
Give me your eyes, listen to my voice &
I'll help you walk"
I just realized why, you show me favor
In a blink of an eye
I'm back eating at that same ol' table
We was having a conversation &
My family wanted to know why I denied you
"I, corrected them & said I love Him"
I'm needing that energy
He got my back even when I'm sipping on Hennessy
He guides my steps
Because I'm an important piece, in his game of chess

7. _You_

I love your soul,
I love your spirit
I love where your reaching
I listen to your words when you are speaking,
you are my rib
Rejoicing over lessons you're teaching
I love,
I love your smile
I love your light,
because living in the dark isn't right
I love your eyes,
A pair given to me by God
Kuz he knew his son was blind
I love…..you
A woman who hasn't lied, since the beginning she's
been…...you
How can words express my love,
countless kisses and hugs that come from….you
Heart pounding, words gibbering,
Just because I'm around…..you
Why are my hands sweating?
My pen rejecting words, kuz I feel I can't make a
perfect poem for…..you
Tears falling down my cheek, my legs are weak
Just because I can't touch….you
You're a picture, perfect moment captured for my
lifetime
You are the oxygen giving breath to my last lifeline

Our love will age, like fine aged wine
What is love?
Is it an emotion?
A natural instinctive state of mind
Is it a feeling?
A belief, especially an irrational one
Or is it in the pit of your stomach
& the energy goes off when they come
To be honest I fell in love with your energy
before….you
Your energy knocked down walls that couldn't be
broken before I met…..you
Your energy danced with my soul for an eternity
before i met...you
Our first encounter was when we were two birds,
perched in a tree
Looking over Adam & Eve
You was hurt
Because that was a relationship you thought
couldn't be deceived
You looked over your wing & flew away when you
saw ...me
It hurt because I didn't get a chance to chirp
It got worse when God I cursed
& He promised I wouldn't see you for centuries and
when I finally do it would be worst for….me
The next time I saw you,
You were a fox & I was a bloodhound
During America's Slavery
God's promise to me, was facts
Kuz you couldn't stand the sight of...me
In the woods you roamed free,

Being a bystander, you were watching....me
Ripping & tearing apart different families
The pain in your face,
Made me make a huge mistake
I turned & bit my master, so he,
Beat me taking my eyes to see
I wept & wept, then took that forever...sleep
Centuries later, I wake up in a hospital
Sensing a familiar energy
Just then I see a beautiful Queen
Long hair, maybe 5'1, Yah can this be...she
Yah give me a chance to be a man for....she
& our daughter, they'll never have to fear
around...me
My love for you runs so...deep
& now our energy can dance...free
I went through centuries trying to find you
So don't ever forget it's been promised we'll always
...be

8. _ThugLife_

Tired of hearing, my circle getting hurt
because their close ones are getting killed
The streets are quenched through blood being
spilled
Circumstances young brothers and sisters got to
live
Because The.Hate
Keeps them hungry, wanting a mill
Looking around, their families stomach they want to
fill
The.Hate.U.Give
Was foretold back in 1994
In 2019 you see, this attention even more
Father's no longer really in homes
Mothers working 1 to 2 jobs, leaving their kids
alone
The.Hate.U.Give.Little.Infants
Love is missing
Mama out here stripping,
Daddy out here pimping
They weren't watching,
giving us no other option
But to watch ourselves
The images they give, make us hate ourselves
The help we need is not considered by anybody,
kuz
The.Hate.U.Give.Little.Infants.Fucks.
Everybody

12 to 13 year olds hitting armed robbery
You find yourself looking into the muzzle of a cold
shotty
These youngins go by any means to get it
THUGLIFE!!!
Is what you gave, so they live it
You want to know the mind of
The.Hate.U.Give
You want to know the action of
The Hate.U.Give
I see it in your eyes
You blame your actions for selling yourself
Short to daddy
That's why, every so often I see you look at me
crazy
Some days you say you love me,
Your eyes some days say you hate me
Misplaced hatred, on why you didn't make it
The reason you didn't go to college with your
friends...but
Had to shake ass to make ends....meet
You lost your innocence when you had to feed...me
The hate you gave showed on many dinner plates
My heart grew cold on nights you didn't embrace
Dreams I had, you told me I couldn't chase
Never preparing me, for obstacles I would face
Girlfriend just texted me, I'm late

9. *Disconnect*

Phone Rings

Her: Hello
Him: How have you been?
Her: What do you want?
Him: What I want is for you to stop turning my
dreams into nightmares
The moment i see your Egyptian queen ass
We get kicked out & the safety of the garden is now
what we're needing

Her: sarcastically laughing

phone disconnects

Him: What I really wanted to say is that I miss you
everyday.......
Him: Hello

Dial Again

Him: Hello
Her: What do you mean I turn your dreams into
nightmares?
Him: Check this out
        You & I, are giving us another try
We at the park & I'm teaching your lil one how to
ride a bike

Smiles on your face, because we no longer fight
The seed I planted, became a flower, you keep
nourishing everyday
I understand, I pushed you to the edge where now
you have a child
But instead of three in this dream we have a family
of four
We at a point in life, you forgave me for everything I
did before
Our future together has no question, this is a for
sure
Somewhere in the distance I hear a roar
three motorcycles riding up a hill with guns,
Just in that moment I knew who they were there for
Baby how could you, I thought you forgave me for
all my mistakes
(Girl: Mistakes, nigga mistakes, you let other
women think they can take my place)
The motorcycles were getting close, on my legs
was 500 pound weights
Trying to run, dragging these weights across the
grass
Looking up, I see a flash, then I hear a blast
Feeling that bullet woke me up so fast....
But regardless the reason

phone disconnects

Him: What I'm trying to say is... I love you
& I'll be your black Ted Mosby
where I'm talking to our kids, telling them our story
of "How I Got Back With Your Mother"

& we'll be sitting there for 10 plus seasons....

phone rings

Him: Hello
Her: Nigga I'll tell you the reason, having me believing, you would never be leaving
AND THEN you leave me for another bitch nigga you sorry, stop calling my phone on this bullshit

Clicks

10. *Love Jones "Butterflies"*

Let's dissect, this insect in my stomach
6 legs, crawling to the words you said
A surgical knife to cut it down the middle
Because I'm looking for its heart
Why does this earthly caterpillar crawl to you?
What picks you apart?
Maybe the locks that lock your poetic energy
Making you live through the pain & joy of poetry
This journey, done gave you a new walk
Changed the uniqueness of the way you talk
A queen of 10,000 moons will light up any room
Recognize she is the earth because of her womb,
ummmmm
Just imagining what I would do from midnight to
noon

Love Jones
I got a Love Jones
I got a Love Jones
For you

Now don't get it twisted, let's get realistic
This creature builds a cocoon to all
No matter how awestruck or what he just saw
He hiding in a place of comfort
She not trying to give any effort
He in a relationship, where he can't tolerate
She's in a relationship, where she don't elevate

Both parties will not participate,
stuck to union mistakes
Olde's given to ex's that left holes
She kinda wants things in an instant
He can only offer distance, where time is different
He is in her future, she three hours in his past
But...what if this is poetry's orgasmic relationship,
these two must have

Love Jones
I got a Love Jones
I got a Love Jones
For you

I'm the brother in the night,
residing in your left thigh,
trying to be the funk in your right
That protective wall now broken
From the wreck & havoc,
a new creature has been woken
No longer will rules of gravity apply to this reality
These butterflies, floating carefree in the wind
Soaking this experience as friends
Helping each other wounds mend
Girl, why pretend our mind won't perfectly blend
Ummm, there goes the skip
Your skip, my skip
Two heart beats synchronized as one
Opening this door, we don't know what just begun
Started communicating in poetic tongue

Love Jones

I got a Love Jones
I got a Love Jones
For you
Me & Mrs. Jones got a thing going on

11. _Nightmare_

I'm in this convenient store
7.50 was all I needed to get out the door
Swishers & Backwoods, so we can roll our dro
The homie grabbing snacks, for the effects,
you know
He told me, about a situation he had to end on the
low
It had to do with a Draco, with an extended mag,
he had to let go
See my homie from the city, where they say got red
snow
T.V news captures the gritty,
Folks mourn the ones that's no more
He told me the story, no questions were asked
They thought he was lacking,
His buddy was the first thing he grabbed
Not thinking of any consequences,
Everything happened so fast
Someone's son or brother was left in the grass
It might end up on the news,
but the police won't catch his ass
They caught him once,
he said that that'll never happen again
Next thing that came out of my mouth,
Nigga you better protect your daughter
I don't want another black girl growing up without a
father
Living in a concrete jungle, it's hard to survive

Do what you got to do, but your fam needs you
alive
In his heart he tries to be a better person
his ears hear it's not working….
Different folk go through different trials
Shaking the Mike & Ike box down the candy aisle
Where these niggas come from,
they running through the store
One of 'em said, "Yeah that's him for sure."
I'm yelling "Run bruh run", thinking why is my body
froze
He's ducking, they running, my feet won't lift off the
floor
Busting around the corner, he slips
Two niggas in front of him, oh shit
Triggers squeezing, people screaming
Triggers squeezing, I'm screaming…
HE GOT A DAUGHTER
Triggers still squeezinag, people still screaming
I'm still thinking, He got a daughter
His pops wasn't around, he wanted to be a better
father
My mind is pacing, my heart is racing
Looking around, where did these niggas go
His words can't make it, his body is shaking
Why is my brother on the floor
My bruh was looking at me,
His eyes speaking I was right
In the end, he never wanted to be taken from his
daughter's life
YAH, give me a second chance,
I'll push harder & fight

To be the one to give my all,
So, my circle will be alright
He losing sight, why is no one here
No sirens going off, this can't be fair
My eyes are open,
Looking around my room, reaching for my phone
Wait…why am I tripping, why am I sweating
Off a fucked up nightmare

12. *Monster*

I don't know what you see
but when I look in the mirror, I see a monster
Hard headed & don't listen
Never realized time is something I'll be missing
When I was younger it was preached to me to
treasure the precious moments I have
Now I'm older & those moments I'm trying to grasp
Back then I thought time was golden,
nothing would ever change
It was my sunny days,
Then I went through parents divorcing, military
joining, my divorces, life I'm trying, honestly don't
know how many times I've seen my mom crying
See I don't know what you see
But when I look in the mirror, I see a monster
24 hours in a day, I couldn't spare a couple minutes
Giving my attention to women, who like tripping
You sitting in a home, your mind forgetting
Times we'll come over for Thanksgiving
Cooking my favorite meal in the kitchen
Your philosophy I couldn't grip
When you would say me and my father need,
A better relationship
I have to admit,
the definition of love I was still learning
Wheels of time was still turning
I know a poem from me was something you were
yearning

If I recite this to you, you'll probably forget it in the
morning
It's too late, at the age reminiscing on past
mistakes
Grandma are you okay?
When Pops passed, my aunty & uncle passed
that was a question I couldn't ask
When your sisters died
I didn't try to call & say everything will be alright
Relating more to the movie, called "Soul Food"
families splitting up, why the message had to be so
true
To both of my Grandma's
I love you
I'm blessed to say I still have you
The messages you passed down from
kids, to grands and greats
Your bloodline insured we'll be great
I'm sorry I was selfish and reckless with time
My mind rewinds the times I would sit on your lap,
look in your face and see Glory
My mind rewinds the times I would sit on your lap,
& you'd tell me stories
Everyday praying to God giving him all your worries
Strength y'all have, blessings y'all have
Can't imagine things y'all went through....
seen through
Recognizing your will because y'all still here
See I don't know what you see
But when I look in the mirror, I see a monster

13. *I AM A POET*

I am a poet, built from the dirt
I am a poet, who had to learn his worth
I am a poet, understanding the importance of my
work
But being built off dirt is not easy
Believe me, you have to learn how it feels to be
stepped on, played with, tricked
Sold on the idea, I could be a magnificent castle
Built with no hassle, no upcoming delays
Forever I believed I would stay, until that day
I would lose that trust
All it took was somebody not paying attention,
then crushed, it was that easy to break me,
understanding I had no foundation,
no pillars to hold me up
Just in that split second I lost my luck
I Am A Poet, who had to learn his worth
See, from being dirt
to understanding my possibilities took a lot of work
Not just time,
they had to change the thought process in my mind
When you have nothing & you're used to getting
stepped on
coming across a lick, justifying why you can do that
crime
are things you will never forget
Being told you're a king,
doesn't always mean, you believe these things

So, what they did was they sat me down
Making me look at images in my background
& what I found, I was made to be strong
Withstanding emotional trauma,
I was meant to last long
Whatever the obstacle, we just got to move on
However, you do it,
Because Grandpa used to sing ol' spiritual songs
Grandma used to say,
put your face in that book, you can start with
Psalms
Finally realizing my body was made to withstand
storms
It was told to me, when the doctor cut my umbilical
cord
He informed my mom,
the importance of me being born
I AM A POET,
understanding the importance of my work
never underestimating the power behind my words
Yes, I heard the saying "Sticks & stones can break
my bones but words can never hurt me", Lies
Kids getting bullied over the internet,
not physically touched but committing suicide
Sometimes ...Poets don't know
when we are on stage, we hold your lives,
reading off words, we write on these blue lines
My responsibility as a Poet,
is to say what's in my dome,
rather it be a love poem, or a
I Hate You I want to break up poem
I'm standing in front of you here is my heart poem

What I'm trying to say is ...I'm needed
Because I AM A POET

14. _My Fight_

Eyes blurred, but I'm still hearing
the fans cheering, the ref counting
my mind is spinning, wait……
I see him trying to talk, what is he saying?.....
ONE…..
supporter in my head,
screaming there's nothing on this earth,
that can knock me dead
TWO…….
seconds to realize the crowd is not cheering for me
they want me beat, excited to see me on the floor
yelling at the top of their lungs "We Want More!"
THREE………
rounds of pound for pound, I can stand my ground
against any noun, verb, adjective, or simile
I Am Screaming, but the crowd noise is louder,
they not hearing me
FOUR…….
gasps of air, I can't breathe,
looking around in these people's eyes,
I could swear, some of my loved ones don't even
care
FIVE…….
What am I doing?
I got to fight ... and stay alive,
For my passion, wearing every single letter on my
back like it's the new fashion,
Asking… No…

SIX.......
My hands can no longer hold this pen,
to touch the sheet,
where my deepest secrets can be unleashed
SEVEN.......
some folk don't believe
my end destination will be Heaven
The land of milk and honey
Where my wildest dreams are running,
in every direction,
everyday learning a different lesson
EIGHT.......
no longer can I wait,
my map, the road in front of me
believe my life won't end here, YOU HEAR
NINE.......
everything is fine, my mind is cleared
Finally raising,
that one supporter praising,
louder than the millions in the stands
TEN.........
sir you don't have to count again
I got my gloves on, my stance right
This fight I'm going to WIN

15. _Grandma_

Unexpected news pierced my heart on Nov 16th
At an unexpected time, Love was taken from me
The reason I am here, was taken from me
Gospel songs playing, my hands are shaking
Tears are on my cheek

95 years of living I wonder what has she seen
Dec 15th 1924, she was here before
America adopted Martin Luther's Dream
Generations were begat from this Queen
Royal blood is pumping in our veins
I sing, for the memories I had with love
I sing, for the warmth of her hugs,
my protector
No one could try her
I remember in that house
Uncle and Dad were chasing me
Busting out that door from the kitchen,
I see white walls green leaves,
Grandma sitting in her chair
I ran under there, she gave them a stare
& both would not dare, my protector
No one could try her

What a beautiful spiritual being
Blessed on this earth
All of her kids learned their worth
From kids, to grands, to greats

Aweing from the glow in her face
her smiles, her laughs, her strengths
She never judged, when I was weak
She congratulated when goals I reached
Encouraged, when she heard my dream

Sugar, butter & rice
So golden, so sweet
She'll make it any given night
It'll be special for me
Unforgetting, She making soul food
for our family on Thanksgiving
Filling our stomachs, to feeding our hearts
She was Love, She was peace
She was the perfect Grandma for me

Rest In Peace
Juanita Crittenton
1924-2019

16. _**Change**_

I'm dirty, I'm hungry, I'm tired
on the street corner with a sign
saying i need some change
so at times I would
 receive
pennies, nickels, dimes & sometimes
small quarters
where I would lay with my small blanket, tooth
brush, and ripped clothes
but people on the outside looking in will say
that's what I choose
and in the next day i will work on a new sign
trying to make every single letter so fine
still asking for change
but not the coins that sit in your pocket
lay on your dresser, or get off the floor
no because your pockets I've been in
your dressers I've been through and the floor
yea the floor I sleep on every single night
But really it's alright, kuz
I NEED SOME CHANGE
Waking up in the morning ready to fight
Asking when will people do what's right?
My circumstances, has given me chances
For advances, yes money I need
Because I have family back home that needs to eat
Do you know a couple of mothers that can't sleep?
They're worried because their children are in these
streets

doing anything to make ends meet
They watching T.V,
seeing brothers & sisters getting slain by police
praying for peace but knowing
we have a problem killing each other in our
community but I know
one day someone will give me my CHANGE
but until that day,
every day I will be on my knees to pray
giving YAH what I can in every way so
let me in my ripped and ragged clothes
stand as this unspeakable homeless man
the only person I know that has done this
is John the Baptist
and if this is true
u can use my body
to feed these onlookers
with my words until they all are so full nothing else
can enter in
then drink the ink off my pen so they're not
thirsty again
and I will give them my all
before my heart, collapse and fall
anytime I have I will stall
my dream is for the whole world to call
my name
The Unspeakable Homeless Man
looking for change
but the funny thing is
I can do all this except bring
Change

17. _A Man_

A man, can be many things on this earth
A father, a brother, a husband, a friend
A provider, a lover, a leader, a.....
Martin Luther King Jr speaker
Malcolm X mover,
To be in the presence of a real man, with Yah on
his side
You can take the essence, to learn, intrigued &
never turn
A man can lead his family to Yah
Such as Jesus showed the disciples the light
As a man responsibility comes in plenty
It's been like this since the beginning,
with Adam & Eve, through time until it reached me
Young man too old
All had a story which needs to be told
A man can be a peace deliverer, a destroyer, a
user, a comforter
As a man we have many titles
The significance of a man you ask,
please read your bibles
Psalms 1:3, tells me
"He shall be like a tree planted by the rivers of
water,
that brings forth its fruits in its season
who's leaf also should not wither &
whatever he does shall prosper"
Ephesians 5:25

"Husbands love your wife as Christ loved the
church & give himself up for her
As a father Ephesians 6:4 says
"Fathers do not provoke your children to anger
but being them up in the discipline &
the instruction of the Lord"
A man's word can cut as deep as a sword
of course, men can do many things
our bloodline runs through kings
A man can give the appropriate gospel
at the appropriate time
A man can change a life, it was done in mine

18. *Feeling Good & Great*

I'm feeling good & great
I have clothes on my back & a smile on my face
Money in my checking & savings
A beautiful woman to satisfy my cravings
What a life, especially if you do right
Living by the laws & staying true to my wife
My daughter is gorgeous, I have to protect her light
I'm feeling good & great
I have clothes on my back & wait…..
Where is the food that's supposed to be on my
plate?
Daughter asking kuz she hasn't ate
she crying & screaming
my phone starts ringing
the bank talking fraud,
someone just hacked my account, I just got robbed
Contemplating about the money I just spent
How am I going to pay this rent?
picking up my girl's phone,
I'm shocked on the text she just sent
I need time to freeze, I need to vent
My daughter stopped moving,
my girl stopped talking,
caught in mid stride 'cuz she was walking,
I'm hearing someone knocking on my door
Opening the door,
to a female I've never seen before
I was in a trance, caught by a glance,

her touch felt like romance
No lie, you'll want again & again & again
Breathtaking, pleasure making
my lady hating, she's facing…...me
watching my climax peak
with an unknown woman who doesn't speak
I can't explain why I feel so free
Her grip got strong, something is going wrong
Her smile was mischievous, snapping her finger my
lady walking to where the dishes is
coming out of the kitchen with a knife
the stranger holding pictures
asking questions like "Do you know who this is?
What about her?"
I had no response to her questions
My wife saying today I'm going to learn my lesson
I look over, the secret woman holding a Smith &
Weston
they start strapping me down in this chair
I'm yelling, "Why the FUCK are you here!"
The woman I've never seen before,
whispers in my ear, "She smells fear."
Showing more pictures asking,
"Isn't it evident, isn't it clear?"
The energy my wife has is anger & disgust
Mrs. Unknown stands up &
says let's discuss
your feelings for your wife when you're alone
Did you show her your phone?
calling ex's, making messes.
When your phone call got disconnected,
she left me a message

your ex wanted you to personally meet me
My wife tells her she can do anything
while taking off her wedding ring
And asked, "Are you feeling good & great?
Are you smiling, with a gun in your face?"
That female asked, "Was it worth it?"
I said, "What!"
She said, "All this drama."
I said, "FUCK YOU!"
She said she was honored
& wanted to meet me personally
as she introduced herself as Karma

19. _On a Second Thought_

"I have stuff on my mind
The stuff that is on my mind is not kind
Let me rewind
Back to the beginning of my thoughts"
That was the intro to my first poem
When spoken word was taught
A time when a young man did not know the
definition of being alone,
before true feelings was ever caught
"I better say what I got to say
Because I may not be here another day
I feel like I'm in a boxing match with my thoughts
They're swinging blows to my chest with no rest"
At 14 I didn't know how to bob & weave
ignorantly putting on boxing gloves,
saying I'm going to fight for my dream,
Not understanding if I get knocked down,
I gotta get up by any means
Naw these were just words,
So, the girl in the front row would take off her
panties for me
Trying to turn a true art to a scheme
Using these words for my needs
"People think I'm lethal,
Even when I walk in these streets with my du-rag &
I sag
People try to judge me
but how the hell can you judge me"

They judge lil man,
because they don't understand
killing a lot of our men,
countless times over & over again
saying it's not racism
can't help to realize it's all because of their skin
They scared of the melanin within
I hear we need to get over it with a smile & grin
"I keep thinking why do I have to act
Like this or that, so I can be called black
That shit is wack"
Being black is not defined by the designer of our
shoes
It's not what they say about us in the news
Being black is the resilience we have with little tools
Being black is when your parents preach,
you have two strikes against you
Being black is walking this earth
knowing you're a spitting image of Yah himself
Being black is accumulating natural wealth
"I refuse to fit into the stereotype
Sometimes my thoughts sink like the titanic & I
panic
Because I got a taste of what the
United Negro College Foundation said,
"That the mind is a terrible thing to waste."
Education is something my brothas & sistas should
all chase
Pharaoh days being educated was in our traits
history books are slowly trying to erase
now pronouncing our words, talking smart
is a white trait

It's time to use our brains, come together
because we all great
I keep hearing let's Make America Great Again
I want to give success to my folk, so we all win
make a new source of wealth,
that won't break or bend
America won't be able to blow to bits.
I'm reminiscing of the desk where I would sit
looking at that poem I had to finish
writing down
"So I keep thinking I should be a young black boy,
getting an education
So when I grow up I'll be grown black man
Getting a promotion
& after all this my mind will be at peace"
them days, them days
I was so young writing on that page
At 14 I didn't know shit
At 14 I didn't know how many times I had to slip &
fall, but I NEVER QUIT
I'm still trying to get that promotion,
In my own way
I'm still being educated
day by day
& my mind is getting to peace
because I pray

Brooks "Poetry" Crittenton
626-860-3642

65359320R00031